the
# Pocket Guide to
# Restorative Justice

*of related interest*

**Restorative Justice**
How it Works
*Marian Liebmann*
ISBN 978 1 84310 074 4

**Just Schools**
A Whole School Approach to Restorative Justice
*Belinda Hopkins*
ISBN 978 1 84310 132 1

**Developing the Craft of Mediation**
Reflections on Theory and Practice
*Marian Roberts*
ISBN 978 1 84310 323 3

**Reparation and Victim-focused Social Work**
*Edited by Brian Williams*
ISBN 978 1 84310 023 2

**Developments in Social Work with Offenders**
*Edited by Gill McIvor and Peter Raynor*
ISBN 978 1 84310 538 1
Research Highlights in Social Work Series

**Constructive Work with Offenders**
*Edited by Kevin Gorman, Marilyn Gregory, Michelle Hayles and Nigel Parton*
ISBN 978 1 84310 345 5

# the
# Pocket Guide to
# Restorative Justice

## Pete Wallis
## and Barbara Tudor

Jessica Kingsley Publishers
London and Philadelphia

First published in 2008
by Jessica Kingsley Publishers
116 Pentonville Road
London N1 9JB, UK
and
400 Market Street, Suite 400
Philadelphia, PA 19106, USA

www.jkp.com

**Library of Congress Cataloging in Publication Data**
A CIP catalog record for this book is available from the Library of Congress

**British Library Cataloguing in Publication Data**
A CIP catalogue record for this book is available from the British Library

ISBN 978 1 84310 629 6

**Note**
The authors have no control over the way in which the information in this
book may be applied in practice and cannot be held responsible in individual
instances for the use of the guidance contained.

Printed and bound in Great Britain by
Athenaeum Press, Gateshead, Tyne and Wear

# Contents

# Acknowledgements

The authors thank Penny Ormerod, Marian Liebmann, Debra Clothier, Roger Cullen, Belinda Hopkins and Alison Williams for their help in producing this book, and all those whose pioneering work in restorative justice has informed this guide. We apologise if it inadvertently borrows from other sources without recognition.

Barbara Tudor is Victim–Offender Development Officer for West Midlands Probation Service.

Peter Wallis is Senior Practitioner (Restorative Justice) with Oxfordshire Youth Offending Service.

Mir Dani (17) painted the cover picture of this book as a gift for the victim of his offence. Mir is a Kosovan Albanian, who chose as his subject a lake that reminds him of home. His victim was delighted with the present.

# 1

# INTRODUCTION

This manual is designed to contain helpful hands-on guidance for restorative processes used in day-to-day practice. It has been produced in response to many enquiries for a pocket-sized guide that can easily be taken on visits or carried into meetings.

We hope it might be useful for:

- Youth Offending Team (YOT) workers
- probation officers
- prison staff
- police
- referral order volunteers

- school or children's home staff
- family group conference facilitators
- community conferencing facilitators
- mediators
- antisocial behaviour order (ASBO) co-ordinators
- in fact, anyone engaged in restorative practice in any field.

This is not an exhaustive reference manual, but it might enable practitioners to feel more confident.

> (!) **Health Warning!** *Facilitating a restorative meeting is a skilled process and should not be undertaken without thorough training in line with current standards. Please use this guide to help you in your practice **after** you have received training (or simply as a reference book if you wish to learn more about restorative justice),* **not** *as an alternative to training.*

The approach we describe here is the criminal justice model. We hope that practitioners in educational and residential settings will find this book useful. However, it should only be used alongside specialist guides for restorative practice in these settings. The restorative process we describe may be appropriate for certain more serious incidents in schools, prisons and care homes. In institutional settings, however, the restorativeness of the whole community is vital to the effectiveness of any single intervention. A range of different approaches, from informal one-to-one conversations, through circle time to the more formal restorative meetings described here, are available.

Many restorative justice schemes use the term 'restorative conference'. We have chosen instead to talk about a 'restorative meeting'. 'Conference' seems rather overbearing, but the guidance contained here is intended for any meeting that brings together a victim and offender, from an informal mediation to a large conference run along more formal lines.

The philosophy underpinning restorative justice is contained in more comprehensive documents elsewhere, some of which are identified in the Resources section at the end of the book. Marian Liebmann's book *Restorative Justice: How it Works* is an excellent resource book on the many aspects of restorative justice. National guidelines on restorative practice can be found in the *Principles of Restorative Justice* (Restorative Justice Consortium 2004) and National Practice Guidelines (Home Office 2004) which link in with the guidance contained here. Restorative practice in a school setting is described fully in *Just Schools* by Belinda Hopkins (2004).

> ⚠ *Throughout this guide the terms 'victim' and 'offender' are used for convenience only. We suggest that in practice these are potentially damaging labels that should not be used when working with clients.*

The restorative process itself tends to be de-labelling, ending, one hopes, with the re-integration of all the parties.

## Introducing restorative justice

Restorative justice is about repairing the harm caused by crime. When an offence is committed, there is a gap between the person causing the harm and those who have been hurt. Western-style justice focuses on punishing the offender, while the victim is often ignored (unless needed as a witness to secure a conviction).

The difference between western-style criminal justice and restorative justice can be shown by an equation. Western-style justice carefully measures the 'seriousness' of the offence, based on the harm caused, and inflicts an equivalent amount of harm on the offender through punishment:

original harm + punishment = harm doubled

The original harm is doubled and the offender is often left feeling that they are the victim. This most often fails to resolve anything for the real victim of the offence. In contrast, restorative justice offers the victim and offender an opportunity to close the gap between them through communication, allowing as much of the harm to be repaired as possible and relationships to be restored:

original harm + restoration = harm reduced or repaired

This way, everyone wins.

In practice, restorative justice feels very natural, and rather like good parenting. If you break something or hurt someone, the important thing is to go to the person affected, explain what happened and why, and explore with them what needs to be done to repair the damage. The offender learns about the consequences of their behaviour and has an opportunity to take responsibility and to make amends. The person hurt may learn why it happened, be reassured that it won't happen again, and gain answers to questions that only the offender can supply. The process itself can feel uncomfortable and there may be strong emotions on both sides. The more serious the offence, the more courage is required for the different parties to come face-to-face. Indeed, many victims state that a restorative meeting is the toughest thing the offender can be asked to do, and frequently it is all that the victim feels is required to put right the harm.

It is amazing how many people are willing to contemplate meeting their offender, and how many offenders are keen to make amends. Seasoned practitioners who have many years of working in caring roles will often say that their experience of a particular restorative meeting shines out as the most meaningful and remarkable encounter in their careers. Extraordinary things can occur in the safe space created by restorative meetings, as people let down the barriers between them and seek a resolution together. Labels disappear and judgement dissolves. As each person's story is told and the participants start to own the process, there is a genuine potential for transformation and healing.

There has been a growing wave of interest in restorative justice in the UK and around the world. Studies find that restorative practices are at the heart of traditional forms of justice in many cultures. It is found in the truth and reconciliation processes in South Africa, East Timor, Northern Ireland and Rwanda. Restorative justice was first introduced in the UK through pilot projects working with adult offenders in the community in the 1980s. The Labour government put restorative justice into legislation for the first time for young offenders with the Crime and Disorder Act (1998) and

Youth Justice and Criminal Evidence Act (1999). More recently, restorative principles are spreading into new areas including schools, children's homes, workplace conflict, bullying in prisons, mental health arenas, neighbourhood conflicts and antisocial behaviour. Restorative justice can be used very effectively to divert people from the criminal justice system (for example, by resolving conflicts in school) but it can equally work in parallel with more formal sanctions, which might be a necessary response for the breaking of societal rules. This is an exciting time to become involved.

As restorative practitioners we work from an holistic standpoint which can appear to be profoundly different from other professionals. We are unable to function without an overview of the whole situation as it pertains to everyone involved. That includes other professional colleagues. Our role is to ensure that our clients understand what is offered and can make an informed and genuine choice about becoming involved. We need to be certain that all parties are fully prepared, and that we are confident in our practice. In a face-to-face meeting we create a safe container, enabling everyone to speak freely, knowing that they won't come to harm. If handled badly there is the potential for restorative interventions to make things worse, and it is therefore in a spirit of learning together and sharing good practice that this pocket guide is offered.

## Principles of restorative justice

The principles of restorative work are of critical importance to the restorative worker. They may seem idealistic, but in practice it quickly becomes apparent that working between people in conflict will always be more complex by its very nature than working with just one party or the other.

Our mantra is that we do no more harm to anyone and enable as much repair as possible in the circumstances in which we are working. As restorative practitioners we quickly become aware that an individual's journey through the criminal justice system can generate more and more damage as their case progresses. The adversarial nature of proceedings makes it necessary to establish 'proven evidence' – frequently something very different to the parties' own perception of 'truth'. Victims often find themselves or their family members spoken of in derogatory terms and emerge from their experiences feeling abused and let down. Offenders may feel that they have been ignored and 'short-changed', pushed through hurdles they were not consulted about and/or did not understand. In the initial stages, they may not feel ready to engage with a process that may prove challenging and demanding. They tend to expect to have further things 'done' to them, not to be encouraged to take a very active and reflective part in trying to seek ways to repair and restore the damage they themselves caused.

It can be challenging for victims and offenders to think through what would be helpful and acceptable in terms of making amends. Tough issues may arise. Does remorse matter? Were others who are known to the participants involved in the crime without their knowledge? What if other friends, family or colleagues 'get to know' about the offence or the restorative process?

Restorative work is a challenge for workers too. You are likely to be handling more information than normal, because you are now working between parties. This will involve skilled interaction and require clear guiding principles.

The fact is that we are always there only to **facilitate communication** by whatever means between others, and this must be made clear to everyone, including ourselves. Tempting as it may often be to 'direct' matters, our role does not allow us to. Inherent in the term 'facilitation' there lies an awareness of the **ownership of the information** that we are in possession of and are entrusted with. The fine line between what is 'confidential' in the strictest sense and what we are charged with sharing, and how we will deliver on that, requires consistent thought and preparation. Everything about ourselves as channels of communication counts – our demeanour, tone, choice of words and timing are crucial in facilitating the exchanges of others.

**Timing** and **pacing** are of prime importance throughout our work. One person will not necessarily be ready to receive information and give it at the same pace as another. Handling that interface to enable everyone to gain the optimum advantage from our work requires an awareness of the issues and positions of all parties, and often their supporters too. In trying to operate at the best time and pace for them, we may also find to our discomfort that we are at variance with other colleagues or parts of the system. We must always remember that our work is '**party-led**'. We are completely guided by the needs, capabilities and wishes of those for whom we work.

**Scrupulous honesty** in our relationships with everyone we work with is essential to their being able to make the decisions they need to. This will help us to manage some of the difficulties we may encounter as we try to fit in with other colleagues, or work around decisions that have been made within the system that may affect what can be achieved. If we let our honesty slip in difficult circumstances, we can be sure that we will be 'found out' and lose the credibility we have to exhibit in order to reach satisfactory outcomes.

Our own **flexibility** to engage with people at different stages of emotional movement helps them to gain the confidence they will need to have in us as they progress through the restorative process. We must be able to offer everyone respect for their position, as well as command their respect for our role. This can give rise to complex situations, especially when we are dealing with oppressive offences such as domestic violence, hate crime and some sexual offences, where there needs to be some rebalancing of power and control in order for effective communication to start.

All parties need to know that they are being 'actively' listened to, a phrase commonly used by mediators and facilitators. **Active listening** involves more than simply concentrating on what is being said. It requires sensitive checking and an exploration of meanings, with care and consideration given to responses and options.

The terms '**neutrality**' and '**voluntariness**' figure large in our vocabulary too. It is simplistic to think that we can always be neutral, especially in the face of some of the more serious offences we find ourselves working with. It would be humanly impossible not to have strong feelings about the appalling suffering that we may witness; but that does not stop us from working in a neutral manner. We can remember the importance of a positive approach in achieving an under-standing of the repercussions of actions, which may not have been evident or considered before we became charged with the responsibility of putting the information forward.

The whole concept of a 'voluntary' interaction informs our work as mediators/facilitators. The difference between the requirement 'you will' and the question 'will you?' illus-trates where our responsibility lies. It is indicative of the need to engage all our consciousness and pacing to enable the tak-ing of full responsibility. In many serious cases it would be useless to state baldly that the victim or victim's relative wishes to meet at the outset of our contact with an offender. Clearly this is a frightening and demanding situation and will feel daunting at the very least. Facilitation does not mean sitting back and 'letting things happen'. It means de-veloping the confidence participants need to engage, con-stantly encouraging their own empowerment and carefully preparing them to think through their capabilities. With en-couragement, individuals can often achieve more than they would have believed at first.

Having proper regard for everyone else's needs also de-mands an ability to attend to our own. It is important that we have the **self-awareness** to step back and take a critical as-sessment of ourselves. We must know how to access support. Every one of us has our own feelings and prejudices of one kind or another. This work, because of its very emotional na-ture, touches nerves in ourselves at times when we may least expect it. We need to develop an ability to address those is-sues that affect us, positively and quickly.

There are some intriguing nuances within this work. We often say 'we are not here to judge', and we mean it, but judgement and assessments are essential and permeate throughout the job. Self-reflection must be taking place con-tinuously, not only to keep testing our competence and resil-ience, but also to ensure that our practice does not become **oppressive** or **discriminatory**. When we are in possession of a whole raft of information coming from many different quarters it can become difficult to operate the necessary bal-ancing act between everyone. It is particularly important when working with young people or those who have been subjected to oppressive crime, that we retain a clear and balanced picture in order to address vulnerability to maximum effect, and ensure that everyone emerges from the process feeling better and more confident.

For the overarching set of the principles of restorative justice, see the Restorative Justice Consortium website, www.restorativejustice.org.uk

## Training, supervision and management

This guide is not a replacement for proper training. Restorative justice training takes typically four to five days and includes experiential and reflective learning, including role-play. Consult the Restorative Justice Consortium regarding the code of practice for trainers, and to access training providers. Ensure that the training complies with the Home Office good practice guidance, and be aware of the complaints procedure run on restorative principles.

- All staff and volunteers (including referral order panel members) should be trained in restorative principles and practice. They should also have experience in working with victims before engaging in restorative work.

- All members of staff and volunteers who facilitate restorative meetings and direct or indirect mediation should expect to have regular supervision, ongoing training and support.

- Communication within your team, with other professionals and with participants is vital to ensure that everyone is on board with the process.

> (!) *All practice with victims, particularly when a restorative intervention is being explored, requires sensitivity and professionalism.*

# 2

## GETTING STARTED

Each case you work with will be unique. There will always be potential for some kind of restorative process, regardless of whether a face-to-face meeting follows. For victims, simply being asked if they would like to be involved may be restorative, as long as the contact is made in an appropriately sensitive and positive way. For offenders, being challenged to consider the consequences of their actions on others will lift them from feeling that they are the victims, and start their process of taking responsibility for their behaviour.

### Taking on a new case

- Before accepting a referral, be sure that you have the time to see the process through. The pace will be set by the participants – you'll need enough time and flexibility in your life to visit all of the parties, possibly several times, and to fit in with their availability so as to ensure that the process isn't delayed because of your own commitments.

- Don't take the case on unless you can give it 100 per cent priority. It may take a lot of time to enable people to feel sufficiently safe and supported to participate meaningfully.

There are lots of potential blocks to the process, which should be allowed to run at the pace of the participants.

- Make sure that it isn't forced to run at your pace, leading to delays which may result in the opportunity for a valuable process being lost.

- Make sure that it isn't forced to run at anyone else's pace, including the system's. There is pressure from the government for the 'swift administration of justice', which can be in conflict with the restorative process.

Offenders will have their own sense and experience of time, and their attitude and readiness to engage may change. Peer pressure might stop offenders admitting to what they have done. Some offenders only start to show remorse a considerable time after the offence – particularly if there has been significant harm. Victims, too, may be helped through a restorative process at differing stages in their recovery. Part of the skill in working sensitively with victims and offenders is to find the right balance between the needs and timings of both parties, so that everyone can benefit.

A restorative process can take place only at a time when both parties feel ready. For probation or Youth Offending Team (YOT) cases, this can be at any stage in the criminal justice process. It is important that 'fast-tracking systems'[1] which focus on speeding up the justice process do not lead either to a rushed attempt to work with the victim at an inappropriate time, or to victims being excluded altogether from the benefits of restorative processes.

- If there is a need to report back to another colleague or agency, report to date and draw attention to any future possible (or definite) actions which are planned. Avoid rushing to a conclusion which might not have the maximum effect for any or all parties.

## Conflict of interest

- Ideally, in a restorative process the only connection between you (the facilitator) and each participant will be to carry out the process.

---

1    See Youth Justice Board (2003a) guidance on fast-tracking.

A caseworker wishing to set up restorative meetings might be best advised to facilitate meetings for offenders who aren't on their caseload. There is a danger that the victims will know that the caseworker is working to help the offender in other areas of their lives, and that this could jeopardise their perception of the facilitator's impartiality. Restorative justice facilitators hold the ground between both the victim and offender, and need to feel comfortable that they are clearly working with and for both parties.

## Continuity

- The relationship you build with each participant is key. Once you take on a case, see it through from start to finish, and undertake all of your own preparatory work.

If anyone becomes involved in the process, it should be made clear in what capacity they are there; if you have a co-worker, it should be stated that each of you is concentrating on the needs of all the parties, and it doesn't mean that responsibility is divided up between you. Participants need to be aware of this multiple responsibility carried by the co-ordinator.

*'My job is to be here for everyone.'*

## Voluntary engagement is crucial

- Ensure that all parties have a genuine choice about whether to participate or not.

- Under no circumstances should any person be coerced into taking part in any restorative process.

- Give accurate and honest information to all participants about the process, outlining both the potential benefits and dangers.

The fact that offenders have actively chosen to be involved indicates to the victim that their participation is genuine.

- There must be no sense for the offender that there is a system pay-off for them in participating – for example, that it will lead to their sentence, community reparation or punishment being reduced. They will, however, benefit personally from addressing the harm caused in a positive way, and by having reclaimed a 'clean sheet'.

## Paperwork – what you need

■ If you are taking on a case as facilitator, don't proceed, or even start to make contacts, without having all the information you require from the referrer.

A pre-sentence report (PSR) or other relevant report about either party (e.g. a school report) is needed. In criminal cases, someone will have completed an assessment of the offender, and the referrer will provide a risk assessment. There may be a victim personal statement. Make sure that the referral forms are completed fully and correctly, and that any potential risk (emotional, physical or practical) is identified.

> (!) *Don't accept the referral unless you have all the information you require in full, and don't give up until you have it!*

**Checklist of information you need before accepting a referral**

✔ Referral form with offender's address and phone number and parental details (in the case of young people).

✔ Victim details, and victim report if initial contact has already been made.

✔ A summary of the offence. This may be an extract from a PSR, referral order report, victim personal report or police case file summary.

✔ Any further information available: e.g. culture, first language, disabilities, etc.

✔ Any further information to inform your own risk assessment.

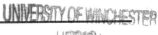

- Don't allow the process to be delayed because you lack a vital piece of information – be persistent until you receive all the information you need to proceed (and alert your supervisor if there is a problem).

- If there are several offenders, check with all their caseworkers to avoid the danger of the victim being approached by more than one restorative justice worker, and to ensure all offenders get the opportunity to participate.

## Keeping a diary

Restorative processes can become complicated by any number of factors. It may be that you have difficulty contacting one or other party.

- Keep a diary of each contact you make. In the event that a restorative meeting fails to take place after weeks of trying to organise one, it is possible that one or other party may make a complaint. A clear diary of each contact or attempt at contact that you have made will help you to provide a clear response to any query concerning your handling of the case.

- Attach the diary sheet inside the front cover of the case record.

## Who to contact first?

Most guidance on restorative practices suggests meeting the offender first. However, as long as the situation is explained clearly, there is no reason why the initial contact cannot be with the victim, as part of a general enquiry about how an offence has affected them. The possibility of indirect or direct mediation can be explored, while taking care not to raise expectations.

> (!) *Regardless of which party you contact first, don't arrange a restorative meeting without:*
>
> - *having met every participant who is to attend the meeting in advance*
> - *encouraging them to think about their expectations and agendas and ensuring that you know precisely what these are.*

# 3

# CONTACTING THE OFFENDER

## Working in partnership with the caseworker

It can't be emphasised too strongly that maintaining a good and clear working relationship with the offender's caseworker is vital. Engaging in a restorative process may potentially be stressful for the offender, and perhaps have a wider impact on his or her life and relationships, so it will be very important to the caseworker to know how things are progressing.

■ Draw on the caseworker for guidance, and encourage them to support the offender throughout the restorative process.

■ Liase with the offender's caseworker to arrange contact, which could be either at the offender's home or in the office. If you plan to visit the offender at home, discuss health and safety.

■ Consider the appropriateness of having the caseworker present and/or a parent or carer if the offender is younger than 16.

Your information about the impact of the crime on the victim(s) and the offender's attitude to their offending may be invaluable to the caseworker in other areas of their work with the offender.

## Home visits: health and safety issues

Before going to anyone's home on agency business:

- Tell someone in your team the address you are visiting (this is not a breach of confidentiality).

- Take a mobile phone and log in (and out). Give a likely time for the length of the visit if possible.

- Have an agreed code to alert colleagues if you need help.

- Have the Social Services emergency duty team number to hand.

- Show your ID card on every visit.

- Refer to your team's local policy for further guidance on lone working and personal safety.

- Don't hesitate to call the police if you need help.

It may be helpful with a complex case, or where there are concerns about safety, to conduct home visits with a co-facilitator. Never be afraid to ask your supervisor or a colleague for help.

> (!) *If you are in any doubt about the safety of a home visit (for example, if it is an isolated area or something makes you feel unsure), don't go into the house. Return and discuss the matter with your supervisor as soon as possible.*

- A home visit to either party may be distressing. Ensure that there is someone you can phone to debrief with immediately after your visit.

## Meeting the offender

Introduce yourself and your role. Be clear what offence you want to talk about with them.

Check whether he or she:

- understands and accepts guilty plea(s)

- agrees with the description of the offence in the pre-sentence report (PSR) or other report
- takes responsibility for the offence

> **When meeting the offender, seek to:**
> ✔ convey a non-judgmental, sensitive approach.
> ✔ establish a relaxed, positive atmosphere.
> ✔ focus on the dialogue between the victim and offender.

Give the offender space to tell the story. Ask a lot of open questions:

*'When did the offence begin – was there any background or build-up to it?'*

*'Why did **you** get involved?'*

*'What did you feel at the time of the offence? Just before? Just after?'*

*'What do you feel about it now?'*

*'How do your family, friends, schoolmates, work colleagues, etc. feel about it?'*

*'Would you do this sort of thing again?'*

*'How does your current position affect the future?'*

It helps to concentrate on what the offender was thinking or feeling, rather than why they committed the offence. The 'why?' question is very threatening.

All the time that you are talking with the offender, drip-feed the victim's story:

*'Do you know the victim?'*

*'Have you seen him/her since?'*

*'What did his/her face look like?'*

*'What did the house/ car/ store look like?'*

*'Who do you think lived in the house?'*

*'Who has it angered? Damaged?''*

*'Who else has it harmed?'* (secondary victims)

*'What do **you** think happened to the victim?'*

*'How do you think they feel?'*

*'How do you think you would feel?'*

Encourage the offender to consider what they might like to do – what options are there?

*'What do you think is going to happen next'*

*'What do you **want** to happen?'*

*'What can you do about it?'*

*'What do you **want** to do about it?'*

*'What would improve things?'*

*'What do you want for the future?'*

A useful phrase to encourage an offender to meet or communicate with the person they caused harm to is:

*'Would you like to meet the victim if it would help them?'*

Explain that a restorative process might help with problems that the victim may be experiencing. Explore their options for communicating directly or indirectly with their victim and describe what the restorative process might involve. Check whether he or she:

- desires to meet the victim or communicate in another way
- understands the process
- understands his or her own role in a restorative meeting
- voluntarily desires to take part in a meeting
- demonstrates capacity to take part in the meeting.

Help the offender to decide whether to participate.

If the offender does wish to take part, encourage him or her to reflect carefully on the crime, prepare what he or she wishes to say about it, and reflect on the victim's experience of the crime. Check whether he or she:

- understands groundrules relating to safe, respectful communication style
- respects the need for safe process
- understands the mediation process and its relationship to the criminal justice or other process (e.g. disciplinary).

Ensure that the offender's expectations are realistic. Allow him or her to select a friend or relative to be a support person at the restorative meeting. If the young person is under 16, it is usual for a parent to attend. Remember to maintain a balance of supporters for both parties, including emotional balance.

- Prepare the offender for disappointment if the victim does not want to be involved. If they are willing to make amends, that is important in itself, regardless of any other outcomes.

## Parents, carers and significant others

- Parents (if the offender is a young person), carers and other supporters should always be invited to participate in a restorative process, whether it is a face-to-face meeting or an indirect mediation. They are an important part of the process and their views are vital. They need to be given appropriate support and information to enable them to participate.

- Assessment of the offender's suitability for restorative work should include the participation of the parents, carers and 'significant others' as well. The offender can be helped to understand the impact that his or her actions have had on them.

- If there is the likelihood of a face-to-face meeting, meet the offender's supporter and parents, carers or significant others in advance.

If this is to be the parents, they may be present at your initial meeting, but ask them to leave if they interfere when you are exploring issues relating to the offence.

## Co-defendants

On occasion, it may be appropriate for offenders who were arrested together for the same offence to take part in a restorative practice together. This may prove particularly helpful to prevent the 'blame' being passed to the absent party.

# 4

# CONTACTING THE VICTIM

Initial contact with the victim may be through a letter, or by telephone.

■ Don't cold call on their house except in exceptional circumstances and after prior discussion with your supervisor.

## Initial contact by letter

Many probation and Youth Offending Teams (YOT) use an 'opt-out' letter to victims, for example when the referral doesn't include a phone number. The letter should suggest an appointment time and ask the victim to contact the team if the time is not convenient, or if they would prefer not to be visited. This may seem intrusive, but evidence indicates a much greater victim involvement with this approach.

■ It is helpful to include an information leaflet with the initial letter to explain the process and services available.

## Possible wording for opt-out letter

Dear

I am writing in relation to a crime that was committed against you in May.

You might like to know that the person who committed the offence is on a court order and is being supervised by this team. Part of his/her order requires him/her to make reparation to his/her community.

Would it be convenient for me to meet you at your home at 5pm next Monday? We would like to learn how the crime has affected you, and to tell you about what this team might offer you.

If you would prefer for me not to visit you, do call. If 5pm next Monday isn't convenient, let me know and I can find a time that suits you better. If I don't hear from you, I'll assume that you would like me to come, and I look forward to seeing you.

Yours sincerely,

## Initial contact by phone

In some cases it may be more appropriate to make initial contact with the victim by phone.

**Before your first telephone contact with the victim, wherever possible you should know whether the offender:**

✔ pleaded guilty to the whole or part of the offence

✔ accepts responsibility

✔ agrees to the facts of the offence – or if his/her version differs, how?

✔ is willing to meet, or make some form of appropriate amends.

During the initial phone call:

- introduce yourself
- check you're speaking to the right person
- ask whether it is a convenient time to talk
- explain your role.

It will be helpful if you can:

- assess the victim's knowledge
- indicate that you have met the offender and mention if they are feeling remorse and would be suitable for a face-to-face meeting

  *'I would like to come to see you and talk about this with you. When will be a good time for me to come and visit you?'*

- make an appointment to meet
- ask whether their supporters might be present when you meet them; this could be a victim support worker/family member/friend, etc.

After this, a personal contact should be made, preferably by visiting them at home.

> (!) *No victim should be made to feel embarrassed or unhelpful if they opt not to be involved.*

If the victim prefers to participate through a third party who can represent their views at a meeting or by another means, such as through a video meeting, this should be made available.[2]

Be prepared prior to making the call for the victim's initial response to be angry. This is perfectly normal; it is rarely personally directed and should be acknowledged as

---

2   Research by the University of Oxford Centre for Criminological Research into restorative cautions given by the police found that 'most of the [non-participating victims] who turned down the chance to meet their offender in a restorative session did so without realising that this is what they were doing… Their understanding about what would happen at the caution was, in most cases, poor' (Hoyle 2002, p.117).

reasonable and to be expected in the circumstances. In general, it is inappropriate to feel (or become) defensive.

- Make sure you have sufficient time to continue with the phone call if the victim finds this a useful time to talk about what happened to them. However, do encourage them to meet with you in person rather than covering everything on the phone, so that you can give them proper attention. If the call is allowed to go on too long the victim may feel that they have said all they wanted to say and decline a home visit. The restorative opportunity may then be lost.

- If you can't answer any questions they may have, do not try to bluff your way through it. Explain that you will make every attempt to find out information that may be available. Explain the parameters of restorative work so that they can keep their expectations in perspective. Undertake to bring all information you can access with you when you call.

- Thank them for their time. If they decide not to meet you and you think it would be useful to share any of the information they have given you with the offender, explain why you would like to and how you will share it. Ask for their consent and check whether they would like any feedback if you do share information from them.

- If possible, attempt to 'keep the door ajar' for communication in case the offender should volunteer information you think could be valuable to them.

## Victim home visit

Victim contact is most helpful when conducted with a personal visit, which will often be most convenient for the victim at their home but can be at any place they choose. Research from Victim Support indicates that victims offered support by phone often don't consider that they have received any support at all; in contrast, those receiving a home visit are far more likely to have felt supported.

- Try to arrange a visit to the victim as soon as possible after receiving the referral, at a time that will suit the victim.

Taking too long to set up mediation when a victim had wanted to deal with it straight away can be as re-victimising as attempting to force them into a process for which they are not yet ready.

> (!) When you visit the victim, you are likely to be the first representative from your agency to enter their property. In some cases even the police won't have met the victim in their home. Follow the guidance for health and safety during home visits scrupulously.

## Victim home visit – health and safety issues

- The police keep intelligence records on names and addresses, and may be willing to share information (for example, if an address you plan to visit is known for drug dealing or dangerous dogs). This may provide a helpful check if you are visiting a victim and have no other information to inform a risk assessment.

## During your first meeting with the victim

When you arrive at the house, ensure that you are speaking with the right person, and then give a clear introduction, state who you are and show an ID card. Check that your visit is still convenient for them. Confirm the identities of all the people there. Provide a brief description of your role and the service your organisation provides.

Listen to their retelling of the story – what happened? Talk about their feelings, both then and now. This may include fear, and self-blame. Initiate a general chat about how things have been for everyone. Who else has been affected?

As you are talking with the victim(s), carefully assess their needs. Affirm their trauma and anger, indicating that this is what the offender needs to hear. You might say something like:

*'I'm here to hear what damage the incident caused and what may be done about it.'*

*'I would like to take some of the things you have told me back to [the offender], with your permission.'*

- Give the victim a sense of the offender.

- Explain what stage the offender has reached in the justice or disciplinary process.

- Consider what it might take to put things right.

- Avoid the temptation to offer excuses for the offender, or to share your own experience as a victim.

- Tell the victim what all the options are, allowing them time to consider whether or not to participate in the mediation process.

- Explain clearly what restorative justice is.

---

**Acknowledgement**

Victims may value:

✔ clear information about their case

✔ a chance to voice their feelings to someone about the offence and its repercussions

✔ a chance to voice their feelings about the offence to the person responsible

✔ having answers to questions like 'Why did it happen to me?'

✔ learning more about the offender/offence

✔ having some form of emotional or physical reparation

✔ being acknowledged as an individual (not a witness)

✔ being encouraged to raise issues about their personal safety.

---

The victim may prefer not to make a decision on the spot. Offer them a leaflet with information about restorative justice, and suggest that they take time to consider their options. Suggest a follow-up appointment for you to hear what they have chosen.

If they are interested in meeting with the offender, give a clear explanation of what the meeting is about:

- Explain that we talk about what happened, who has been affected and how we can repair the harm caused.

- Explain clearly who is likely to be at the meeting.

- Discuss supporters and supporter roles.

- Clarify who will convene the meeting.

- Cover groundrules and confidentiality.

- Ask whether the timing is right.

- Check:

  *'Do you wish to know what questions are likely to be asked?'*

- Ask:

  *'What would you like to see come from the meeting?'*

- Don't raise expectations about outcomes, and ensure that everyone's expectations are realistic.

- Discuss possible date, time and venue, allowing them to choose.

- Stress that their free choice remains open.

If they don't want to meet the offender, do they know of any person who would be willing to attend for them? If not, ask whether they would like you to say anything on their behalf.

- Give lots of time for their questions:

  *'Is there anything you wish to ask me?'*

  *'Have you any concerns?'*

- Feed back and check if it's OK to relate the things you have discussed to the offender and/or caseworker.

- Check out whether you have permission to speak with the others who may have been affected.

Victims may need encouragement to participate in restorative procedures. Making personal contact in a sensitive manner is essential. Expecting victims to respond merely to a written invitation rarely provides sufficient encouragement.

Consider producing a video or newsletter with accounts from people who have been through a restorative process, to help victims in making their choice.

---

**What does a victim require?**

✔ safety

✔ freedom to say no

✔ answers to their questions

✔ a sense of who the offender is

✔ a chance to tell their story

✔ a chance to talk about the harm they and others suffered

✔ an assurance that the offender will listen

✔ sensitive consideration of any cultural and/or disability issues.

---

## Victim Support

■ During your first meeting with the victim, discuss the role that Victim Support plays and provide contact details.

A Victim Support volunteer may be present at any direct meeting with the offender if the victim wants it. Take Victim Support leaflets. A referral to counselling or other services may be appropriate.

■ Collect useful information leaflets and build up a list of local resources. Many victims have poor access to appropriate support and you may be a key broker in linking them up with agencies that can offer help.

## Unanswerable questions

The victim may ask lots of questions that you do not feel confident to answer on the spot.

■ Offer to find out and come back with your answer at a later date.

- As with all your work, be sure to tie up all loose ends – if you offer to do something, make sure it gets done.

> **During the visit, seek to:**
> ✔ instil trust/confidence
> ✔ be honest/respectful
> ✔ inform the victim about the process, roles, and its voluntary nature
> ✔ consider cultural/disability issues.

> ⚠ *Do not attempt to coerce the victim to attend a face-to-face meeting. Equally, don't think that you know what is best for the victim and decide for them. Victims are bolder than we may allow for, if asked in the right way and with the appropriate support.*

## Young victims

- If the victim is under 16 any approach should be made initially through a parent or carer. Some parents/carers may wish to protect their child from revisiting the trauma.

- Consider meeting the parents or carers to help them understand the process thoroughly before they rush into a decision – the young person may be holding in many fears and hurts that perhaps can only be resolved in a restorative process.

- Help the parents or carers to feel recognised and supported themselves as a secondary victim of the offence, which may have been deeply traumatic. If they remain clear that engaging in a restorative process with the offender would be a negative experience for their son or daughter, their decision has to be respected.

- Invite them to attend for themselves and/or on behalf of their child, if appropriate.

On occasion, restorative practices have been successful with significant others, where a parent/carer or young victim hasn't been involved.

## Commercial victims

Many commercial crimes create personal victims.[3] A crime against the proprietor of a local store may affect an individual profoundly, and even jeopardise the business. The sense of invasion and worries about repeat victimisation can be powerful. If this is the case, the victim clearly needs to be treated in exactly the same way as a non-commercial victim.

Offences committed against large department stores or other businesses where it is clear that there has been little or no emotional impact on staff are in a slightly different category, although a restorative process can still be valid and helpful on both sides.

- Explore with the store or company whether there has been someone whose feelings were affected by the offence and who might benefit from the opportunity to express their hurt to the offender. It may be the person who had to clear up a mess, apprehend the offender, account for the loss of earnings to head office, etc.

- If a corporate representative is involved in several meetings (where the store is a repeat victim), try to avoid being over-familiar with them – this will be off-putting for the offender. Meetings which become formulaic, or where the store is too rigid to allow some movement during the meeting, may not be helpful to either party.

- Always try to personalise the offence – the greatest impact for the offender is when it is shown that the offence has had a personal effect on the victim, whoever they are.

---

3 Figures for burglaries, vandalism and theft of or from vehicles show that retailers are far more likely to be the victim of a crime than the public. However, many restorative justice schemes and research studies ignore corporate victims. The 2002 Commercial Victimisation Survey found that three-quarters of all retailers had been a victim of at least one crime over the previous year (Taylor 2004).

## Schools as victims

An offence committed against a school, whether relating to property or against a staff member, may result in particularly intense feelings of hurt and distress, which in some cases can be extreme. The teacher may be aware that pupils are affected as secondary victims. They may feel less safe. They may be denied the use of equipment if it has been stolen or damaged. They may have had to miss lessons as a result of the offence. Many schools have some awareness of restorative justice principles, and a number have been involved with direct reparation and/or community reparation.

# 5

## ASSESSMENT

### Is a face-to-face meeting feasible and appropriate?

■ Having met both parties, and in communication with the offender's caseworker, assess whether a restorative meeting is possible, safe and appropriate.

Recalcitrant offenders aren't necessarily a problem. If the victim is adequately prepared, this won't be a surprise. In your assessment, consider:

■ motives

■ abilities

■ feelings

■ personalities

■ risk, both emotional and physical.

### Risk

Following a successful restorative process, everyone should feel better. Risk, in restorative justice terms, includes the possibility that someone may end up feeling worse, as well as the danger of physical violence. As you consider next steps, balance the potential risk with your ability and experience as a facilitator.

### Written assessment

Many schemes use a written assessment form, which is completed during the preparation stage of the restorative

process. The form can cover emotional and practical risk, provide an assessment of the victim's needs, and indicate the appropriateness of a direct or indirect restorative process.

- Committing your assessment to writing may help to clarify your decisions. It can be shared with your supervisor and maybe useful for reference at a later date.

- Assessment needs to be dynamic, and if circumstances change, you may need to complete new forms.

## Criteria for not proceeding with a direct meeting

There are several issues that may make a direct meeting inappropriate, even if both parties would like it to go ahead. Examples that may make a direct meeting inappropriate are:

✗ if there is a danger that the victim may feel re-victimised by the process

✗ when the time is not right for the victim

✗ when there are unrealistic expectations

✗ when all parties are not fully informed about the process

✗ when it is likely to be done badly through lack of facilitation skills/preparation

✗ when the victim is being used

✗   when there is an imbalance in the number of supporters for each party attending the meeting

✗   when there is total denial of responsibility on the part of the offender

✗   when there is the risk of physical or mental harm

✗   when there are unbalanced power relationships, which cannot be balanced in a meeting.

The restorative justice process is designed to help ensure wherever possible a positive outcome for all participants, including the offender. The dynamics of the process usually ensure that this is the case, although don't expect the desired outcome always to be achieved within the time limits of the meeting. This may not be reached for some time after a meeting. However, if a positive outcome is not reached during the meeting it may be appropriate to try to disassociate the offence from the offender. You could point out that the offender may not be a bad person: it was the offence itself that was bad. This will help to ensure that the offender has a positive outcome.

## Disputed harm

It is not unusual for us to be dealing with cases where it's not absolutely clear who is the 'offender' and who is the 'victim', and where the exact facts of what happened may be murky. In cases where there isn't a clear demarcation of responsibility for the incident, an agreement can be made about which issues will be focused on. The aim of restoring relationships and establishing safety remains the same.

## Confidentiality

Restorative processes should aim to be confidential for all, but in certain cases of child protection and more serious offences, limits of disclosure should be clear, in order to encourage participants to feel able to be as open and honest as possible. Confidentiality should be discussed with all parties in preparation for a possible face-to-face meeting, when agreeing groundrules. However, never promise that the meeting will be fully confidential – you never know what the other participants might say.

- Only pass on information about the victim or offender to the other party if you have gained permission to do so.

- Be aware of the power you have in holding information, and take care about ownership of information.

- Change can come by the handing over of information, but always remember that it isn't yours to pass on without clear and specific permission from participants. Also, it is necessary to seek permission to pass on information to the offender's caseworker.

- If either party does reveal some cause for concern, explore with that person whether they would like you to support them in taking appropriate action.

---

(!) *Don't tell either party where the other party lives (it may be that they already know, which is fine). Either side may choose to use their first name only to protect their identity.*

(!) *Never give out your own home phone number or address.*

# 6

# AGREEMENT TO MEET

It isn't uncommon for one party or the other to change their mind about meeting, possibly because circumstances have changed or they have begun to feel uneasy about the prospect.

- Reassure the participants that they can withdraw or rejoin at any stage of the process.

## Multiple victims and co-defendants

- If there are several victims of an offence, make an assessment about whether it is appropriate for all to be offered a chance to meet the offender, either as a group or during separate meetings. Equally, if the offence was committed by a group, decide whether it is appropriate for the victim(s) to meet with all the offenders at once.

In general, it is important to get a rough balance of numbers between the parties at a restorative meeting. If there are several victims or several offenders present, invite the opposite party to have more supporters at the meeting so that they don't feel outnumbered. Try to find a family member or someone they get on with, or perhaps suggest inviting Victim Support or the offenders' case holder, to create a better balance.

## Safeguards for young and vulnerable victims or offenders

> (!) *Involvement of young people of 16 years and under may only be arranged with the consent of their parents or guardians, who should be given the opportunity to participate.*

### Learning styles and needs of young people

Many offenders have particular barriers to learning that may affect their ability to benefit from some restorative interventions.

- Ensure that you have relevant information from the assessment profile and other sources, and that this is taken into account in making decisions about appropriate restorative work. In particular, some offenders may have levels of literacy and/or difficulties with speech and language that inhibit their ability to:

  - assimilate written information

  - write letters of apology

  - express their thoughts, feelings and views orally

  - sustain a conversation.

The possibility of a meeting with the victim, the format and groundrules, need to be clearly explained in simple language.

Direct meetings should take into account that some young people in particular have limited attention spans. As the length of any restorative meeting is roughly proportionate to the number of participants, consideration should be given to the number of supporters attending.

- Ask the caseworker and other professionals for guidance on how to approach the offender's needs.

- Prepare the victim so that they are aware of what to expect.

Any help to maximise the opportunities of the restorative process should be harnessed. This may rest with others in the community or colleagues from your team, and indeed with some other participants in the process. As long as these issues are dealt with sensitively, any help to achieve a good experience should be utilised. The responsibility for this lies with practitioners.

## Cultural issues

Often the cultural backgrounds of victim, offender and staff are different, which might lead to miscommunication, feelings of being misunderstood, or even re-victimisation. There is also a danger of over-generalisation – there are as many differences within cultures as between cultures.

Differences between people raised or living in different cultures are often reflected in differing communication styles, including eye contact, body movements and posture, as well as variations in the use of language. Mediation will be more successful when facilitators are aware of the potential dangers and understand how differences in communication styles can lead to miscommunication, which defeats the restorative justice process.

**It may help to:**

✔  reflect on one's own behaviour, communication styles and 'cultural baggage'

✔  refrain from making quick assumptions about others

✔  perceive the participants as individuals within the context of culture, noting how they see the world

✔  nurture relationships with individuals in an unfamiliar culture or community

✔  prepare the participants in restorative justice by helping them understand the viewpoints and different communication styles of other participants.

## Equal opportunity for all

A key restorative value is an acceptance of diversity. Give thought to ensure that your service is accessible to all. Address the needs of those for whom English is not their first language, the less literate, those with auditory or visual challenges, and the less able-bodied.

- Consider Braille and sign language provision.

- Make necessary provision for people with physical disabilities.

- If either party requires an interpreter or other aid to communication, this should be arranged in discussion with the caseworker. Written information can be translated.

## Keeping both sides informed

Working at the pace of the victim can make the process a long one. In some cases, the procedures may go on for months.

- Keep both sides informed through phone calls, visits and letters.

# 7

## PREPARING FOR THE MEETING

### Venue

- Give the victim an opportunity to choose the venue. This may be their own premises (home, school, shop, business, etc.) which in some cases will be an appropriate choice. However, it is important that the venue is fully agreed by both parties so that everyone feels safe and comfortable.

- Make arrangements for people with disabilities, remembering the need for privacy and dignity.

- Explore venues with a 'loop' system for the hard of hearing, or arrange Braille provision where appropriate.

- Send a map and a clear letter to both parties, followed up with a phone call.

- Make sure that transport is sorted out. Phone the evening before and on the day if you are anxious, and arrange to give anyone a lift if that will help. Remember to offer to reimburse travel and other expenses.

It will be re-victimising for the victim if the offender fails to attend, and disappointing for the offender if the victim does not show.

---

> ☐ *Don't let problems negotiating with a particular venue delay the process – find an alternative.*

---

- Consider the number of rooms you will need. It might be important to have several rooms available for final preparation or debriefing of different parties, and to allow you to stagger arrivals and avoid chance encounters before the meeting. If you have a co-facilitator, you can decide in advance who will welcome each party.

## Co-facilitation

- It is good practice to co-facilitate a restorative meeting with someone who has been trained. Advantages of co-facilitation include:

  - safety for participants and co-facilitators

  - mutual support

  - post-meeting debriefing

  - participants' rapport with one or both facilitators

  - provision for diversity in:
    - communication styles
    - facilitation styles
    - culture, gender, age, etc.

  - complementary skills

  - division of tasks

  - sharing responsibility (difficult cases)

  - learning from one another (apprenticeship)

  - modelling co-operation and respect

  - supervision

  - quality assurance.

## The room

- Arrive half an hour before the meeting, so that you don't feel rushed, can set out the room and refreshments, and be sure you are there before any participants.

- Make sure there is a box of tissues available.

- It can be helpful to have a low coffee table, perhaps with glasses of water or flowers on it, in the centre of the circle. This can give participants something to look at during the meeting and make the experience of facing the other party less threatening.

- Invite the parties to come at different times to avoid accidental meeting beforehand. It may be best to settle them in separate rooms prior to the meeting.

- Make sure that you can offer tea and biscuits, without having to leave the room to search for these.

## Seating

Seating may best be arranged in a circle. Think carefully in advance who will sit where. It is usual to have the main victim and perpetrator in positions so that they can face one another without turning. They may wish to have their supporter(s) beside them.

If each has a supporter, consider an 'X'-shape arrangement, with the victim facing the offender's supporter and the offender facing the victim's supporter. The offender and victim can readily make eye contact, but aren't sitting directly opposite one another.

Typically the two facilitators will be opposite one another.

- Whatever arrangement you choose, think carefully about seating and eye lines.

## Health and safety at the venue

- Be aware of exits in the event of an incident, and be sure that you know about fire procedures and exits.

- Check that the venue has public liability insurance (ask to see their certificate). They may also have a written risk assessment.

- Plan for risk, considering seating arrangements, furniture, alarms and pagers. Arrange for assistance from a colleague, if necessary, and for refreshments and breaks.

- Put a *'Meeting – please do not disturb'* sign on the door.

## Restorative justice in custodial settings

Some offenders begin to express remorse during their time in custody, and it may be a fruitful time to begin a restorative process. The gap between the victim and offender is likely to be most extreme (both physically and emotionally) where the perpetrator of an offence is in prison. During this time, indirect or direct reparative work may be most beneficial. When the offender is preparing to return to the community, both parties may be anxious about bumping into each other in the community, and a restorative process may help reduce fear and anxiety.

If a restorative meeting is to take place in a custodial setting, it is important that you:

- fully brief custody personnel about the restorative process, etc.

- extensively brief victims as to what to expect in a secure environment

- outline security procedures to the victim and supporters, including searches (if appropriate), ID requirements and banned items

- find a venue within the prison that is secure, but that allows the victim to feel as comfortable as possible

- arrange a visit for the victim, if possible, beforehand.

The prison chaplain may have a room that would be suitable. Probation may also be able to help.

## Arrival of participants

Remember that it really does take a lot of courage to attend a face-to-face meeting of this nature.

- Take care in welcoming the participants and be aware of how anxious they may be feeling on arrival.

- Show the victim/s into the room first and make sure that they are comfortable.

- Make sure facilitators have a chance to see all participants immediately prior to the meeting.

- Consider the needs of participants who have travelled a long way to attend.

You may also be feeling anxious. Well-planned meetings reduce anxiety. Keep calm and display a caring, responsive attitude toward participants. Do not flap or fuss, even in the face of unforeseen events. The well-being of participants is dependent on your good management. Remain flexible and always be prepared for the unexpected.

---

**Remember to bring:**

✔ mobile phone for health and safety back up

✔ tissues

✔ flowers

✔ paper and pens for contract

✔ facility for copying contract

✔ flipchart with pens for groundrules

✔ tea, coffee, sugar and milk

✔ jug of water and glasses

✔ 'Do not disturb' sign

✔ food, if anyone has come a long way to attend.

# 8

# DURING THE MEETING – ISSUES

## Silences
During the meeting, don't be afraid of silences.

- Wait for the person to reply and don't fill the gaps.

## Client-led
In the early stages of the meeting participants naturally will spend time looking at the facilitator.

- Use your own body language to encourage eye contact between the parties.
- As the meeting progresses, you may want to slide out of the circle a bit.

## Accept ambiguity
Sometimes in a conflict the identification of fault is unclear; we may have to accept ambiguity.

- Encourage people to take as much responsibility as they can for their part in the conflict. Not all conflicts will be fully resolved.

## Neutrality
Neutrality as a restorative justice facilitator means remaining detached from outcomes. Like the process itself, outcomes belong to the parties who have been involved. It also means being there for the benefit of both parties. It is difficult to

assess outcomes that may be very personal to participants, and can emerge over time.

- Try to be non-directive, and not to lead or to follow your own agenda.

## Strong emotions

It is normal for participants at a restorative meeting to get emotional, and an open expression of anger is healthy, providing everyone is prepared and feels adequately supported. Victims need to have their feelings heard and acknowledged, and once that is done meetings often reach a turning point, where the focus becomes one of re-integration for the offender. At times you will have to keep your nerve to avoid jumping in and suppressing that expression.

- If you judge that the participants' emotions are strong and may be overwhelming, it's advisable to meet with people more during the preparation stage.

- If you feel that someone is being attacked personally, gently remind everyone of the agreed groundrules.

- If, during your preparation for a meeting, you anticipate very strong feelings, it may be best to write the groundrules down on a flipchart.

- You may find it helpful to remind everyone that it is the behaviour that is being judged, not the person.

- Keep checking on everyone's thoughts, feelings and needs throughout the meeting.

> ⚠ *If a meeting is becoming too heated, suggest time out.*

## Scripts

Some models of restorative meetings work to a fixed script for the facilitator to follow. Whereas it may be helpful to have some prompting questions ready, it is important to remember that some participants may need little or no assistance to engage with one another. Others will need more structure. The prompts contained in this guide may be useful to you and some are adapted from the script first devised by Terry O'Connell in Australia (O'Connell, Wachtel and Wachtel 1999), but beware of becoming too rigid in your practice. Don't forget that the meeting belongs to the participants.

## Language

Keep your language simple and direct, and avoid slipping into jargon. Take care to adapt your words to the situation; speaking of 'repairing the harm' may not be appropriate for a grave crime where repair simply isn't possible.

# 9

# THE RESTORATIVE MEETING

A restorative meeting naturally progresses through a series of stages. It is vital that the facilitator is aware of where the participants are in the restorative process and that they bear in mind the restorative principles at each stage. Following introductions, welcomes and groundrules, the focus may start with the past, exploring thoughts and feelings surrounding the offence and establishing what harm was caused. The meeting may then progress through the present, hearing how people are feeling now, and considering what is needed to put things right, and finally look ahead to how the situation can be avoided in future.

- Give sufficient time for each stage. Check with your co-facilitator (if you have one) to ensure that everything has been fully explored before moving the meeting on to the next stage.

The following model suggests five stages in the restorative process, but the key is always flexibility. We offer some prompts, many of which are adapted from the restorative conference script, but you will certainly develop your own style.

## Summary of stages
**Stage 1**: Introductions and groundrules
**Stage 2**: Hearing everyone's stories
**Stage 3**: Addressing issues and needs

**Stage 4**: Reflecting on ways of repairing the harm
**Stage 5**: Endings

> ☐ *Facilitating a restorative meeting is a skilled process and should not be undertaken without thorough training!*

## Stage 1: Introductions and groundrules

The first stage of a restorative meeting can be over in a flash, or it may take 15 or 20 minutes, depending on the situation. In an informal mediation between people who know each other and are keen to restore their relationship, you may be able to dispense with introductions and groundrules. For a meeting where participants are anxious and emotional, it may be helpful for them to have quite a long period at the start of the meeting when only you are speaking. They can acclimatise to the room, centre themselves and have space before the spotlight falls on them to speak. You may notice them surreptitiously glancing at the other party from the corner of their eye.

■ Be flexible to need, and avoid giving the impression that you are going through a mechanical checklist.

### Names

■ Prior to the start of the meeting, ask how everyone wishes to be addressed.

> ☐ *Take careful note of, and remember, everyone's name.*

■ Ask for mobile phones to be switched off (and make sure yours is off too!).

■ Don't forget health and safety and domestic notices.

  *'Please turn your mobile phones off. The fire exits are…and the toilets are located…'*

Introduce yourself first. It is usually best to introduce each participant and indicate their reason for being here, rather than ask them to say who they are.

*'Welcome. As you know, my name is...'*

*'Before this meeting begins, I would like to work my way around the group...'*

## Groundrules

■ Although the question of groundrules will have been raised with both parties during preparation, discuss and agree them with all participants at the start of the meeting so that they can feel safe.

You must do what is needed to create a 'safe container' for the participants. If you anticipate a challenging meeting, take more time establishing groundrules, possibly even writing them on a flipchart so that they can be referred back to if needed. The bottom line is that the meeting must feel safe for all parties, both physically and emotionally.

One common groundrule is that, while the expression of emotion is actively encouraged, this must only be done through language that is respectful. Another is that no participant will interrupt another.

*'Everyone will be given an opportunity to have their say.'*

*'Listen respectfully if someone is speaking.'*

*'Don't interrupt, or use abusive or threatening language or behaviour.'*

Stress that anyone may call a break at any time during the meeting, and be ready to suggest one yourself should things become heated or if someone is distressed.

*'Take time out if you need to.'*

Encourage everyone to be open and speak truthfully. Honesty will feel like medicine, but if either party is clearly lying, little may be achieved. A sudden disclosure can completely transform a meeting.

*'It's taken a lot of courage and effort for us all to get here, but the meeting will be pointless if we don't speak truthfully.'*

The limits to confidentiality are best covered in preparation, rather than in the meeting itself.

*'Are we all agreed that what we share today will remain private and confidential? We all must feel sure that nothing will go outside this meeting unless we have all agreed that it should.'*

- Check that everyone understands and agrees with the groundrules, and ensure that they have had a chance to add their own, should they wish to.

*'Does this seem fair to everyone?'*

## Setting the Scene

If necessary, *briefly* explain how the meeting relates to the formal process of caution/court/disciplinary, etc., using simple language. Focus the meeting on the particular incident that brings everyone together, and state again that each person has come voluntarily, if that is the case.

*'The meeting will focus on the incident that happened ... [time, date, place, brief description].'*

*'It is important to point out at this stage that you all freely chose to be here today.'*

Remind everyone that the offender accepts responsibility. Establish that the focus of the meeting is on exploring how everyone was affected by the incident, and on repairing the harm that it caused.

*'[Offender] [4] has admitted [his/her] part in the incident. It is important that we all understand that this meeting will focus on what [he/she] did and how [his/her] behaviour has affected others.'*

*'You will be able to explore in what way people have been affected and, we hope, work towards repairing the harm that has been done.'*

You may like to stress that it is the behaviour rather than the person that is unacceptable.

*'You are not here to decide whether anyone is a good or bad person.'*

*'We all make mistakes. It's how we deal with them that matters.'*

> (!) *At all times keep your use of language simple and check everyone's understanding.*

---

4   There may, of course, be more than one offender and several victims.

Be sensitive to attention spans, cutting short your introduction if eyes are glazing over.

## Stage 2: Hearing everyone's stories

Throughout Stage 1 you have done most of the talking. Now it is important to stop! Remember that this is **their** process, not yours. You are simply providing that safe container to enable communication.

You may like to briefly outline the structure of the meeting, and reassure everyone that they will all have ample opportunity to speak.

*'After everyone has had a say, I will make sure you all have a chance to ask questions or respond to what others have said.'*

### Exploring the impact of the offence

This part of the meeting is critical. Encourage the offender to answer your questions as fully as possible.

- Let awkward silences develop if the offender isn't responding or is monosyllabic. Avoid rescuing them by skipping to another question too soon.

Start with the offender's story.

*'Shall we start with...[offender]?'*

- If you wish to, show respect by checking that the victim is happy for you to start with the offender.

  *'Is that okay?'*

The offender may launch straight into a blow-by-blow account of the incident, which may be fine. However, knowledge of eveyone's agendas is key. In some cases, establishing exactly what happened is what the victim needs. In others, it is more important for the offender to express what they were thinking and feeling at the time and to share how they feel about the offence now, rather than establishing the exact 'facts'.

Focusing on thoughts and feelings may be helpful to steer a meeting away from sliding into a nit-picking argument between victim and offender about precise details that may in any case be disputed. It makes it less likely that the offender will attempt to minimise their actions or even shift the blame. What isn't in dispute is that they have done something that they acknowledge was wrong, and that the victim has been harmed.

*'What were you thinking at the time?'*

*'How were you feeling?'*

*'What have been your thoughts since?'*

*'What are your thoughts now?'*

*'How do you feel now?'*

The offender should always be asked to explore who he/she thinks is likely to have been affected by the incident.

*'Who do you think has been affected by your actions?'*

■ Make a mental note of their response for later.

Keep the focus on the offender until you are satisfied. A degree of discomfort is normal.

*'Thank you for what you have told us. We will now find out how your actions have affected...[victim] and others. I will come back to you and give you a chance to respond to what they say.'*

The victim may jump in at any point during this stage of the meeting. They may speak directly to the offender with a challenge, statement or question. You need to judge whether the interruption is taking the meeting in a positive direction. If it clearly isn't helpful, gently remind the victim of the groundrules and reassure them that they will have an opportunity to speak in a moment. On the other hand, the victim may take control of the meeting entirely, and you may decide to gently move your chair back a few inches and let the participants get on with what they need to do.

■ Remember to pay full attention to what is being said throughout.

■ Your body language is important. Avoid slouching, and show curiosity about what is being said.

## Clarifying the consequences for the victim

When it comes to the victim's turn to speak, ensure that you draw out their story fully so that everyone understands the emotional, physical and material costs that they have suffered.

*'How did you find out about what happened?'*

*'What were you thinking at the time?'*

*'How did you feel?'*

*'What have your thoughts been since that time?'*

*'How do you feel now?'*

*'What has been the hardest thing?'*

> ☐ *Avoid answering the question for the victim. It is so easy to follow an open question ('How did you feel...') with your own reply ('It must have been terrifying') before they can get a word in.*

## If communication falters

Gesture and tone of voice will encourage and ease participation. If communication falters, bland comments can restart the discussion.

*'It's hard...'*

*'Mmm...'*

Deliberately concentrating on your shoes can be enough to prompt participants to pick up the threads of the dialogue themselves.

## Ripple effects

You can remind the meeting about the offender's idea of who has been affected by the incident, and then invite the victim to add to the list. This is a powerful way of demonstrating the ripple effect of crime and acknowledging the harm suffered by others who may not be present.

*'Who else has been affected?'*

## Hearing from the supporters

Go around the room asking similar questions of the victim's supporter(s), followed by the offender's supporter(s). Make sure that everyone has a chance to speak fully and share their own story. Invite each to add to the list of secondary victims.

The victim's supporter(s) may be able to elaborate on the effect on the victim.

*'Have you been aware of any effect on...[victim]?'*

The offender's supporter may have had an awful time themselves. Solidarity may develop between the different supporters (particularly if they are all family members) as a result of their common suffering.

■ Take care, especially in larger meetings and family group conferences, to avoid momentum building up, with participants ganging up on the offender(s).

## Stage 3: Addressing issues and needs
### Identifying specific needs arising from the offence

The meeting may serve to highlight specific needs of victims and offenders which may not have been known or accepted before. Restorative interventions take place in a multi-agency framework, and during the meeting support for either party can be identified. If information about or referral to other agencies is relevant, discuss thoroughly with participants after the meeting, and either give information or make arrangements as appropriate.

### Victims' questions

The victim may have specific questions that they need to ask the offender. If they raised issues during preparation that haven't surfaced during the meeting, it may be appropriate to gently remind the victim and ask whether they would like to raise them now. Restorative meetings usually only happen once, and it is important for all parties to get what they need.

Throughout the meeting, keep alert for statements, questions, issues, etc., which are raised, and if appropriate draw the meeting back to address them at a later stage.

## The offender's response

When everyone has spoken fully about the impact of the offence, return to the offender. If the meeting has heard about significant trauma caused by the offence, you might say:

*'That must have been difficult for you to hear.'*

Invite the offender to respond.

*'You have listened to everybody and heard how they have been affected by what you did and the harm it has caused. Is there anything you wish to say?'*

## Apology or no apology

The offender may spontaneously apologise. However, they may not, and many successful restorative meetings achieve a good outcome without a spoken apology. The victim may get everything they need from an explanation, answers to burning questions, offers of reparation, or reassurance that it won't happen again.

> ⚠ *Don't tell the offender to apologise! If they do apologise it may be perceived as insincere because it wasn't spontaneous. If they don't, you will have raised the expectation, and the victim may feel angry and aggrieved that the offender refuses to say sorry.*

## Stage 4: Reflecting on ways of repairing the harm

Encourage the offender to consider how they might repair the harm. Try to avoid feeding them ideas – they may come up with something unexpected and creative.

*'You can see the harm that the choices you made have caused. Is there anything you could do to help?'*

It may be that we are aware of something the offender said outside the meeting that might be helpful.

*'Do you remember when you were telling me about...'*

## Practical reparation

All research shows that it is the communication that is appreciated by most victims, and not the receipt of material reparation. However, the victim has an opportunity to ask for practical reparation, and a piece of work by the offender to repair the harm can be of real value. A small task may be more valuable than a calculated number of hours. The offer of something practical can of itself be restorative.

## Proportionality

The amount and duration of practical reparation shouldn't be excessive in proportion to the harm caused.

- As meeting facilitator, you may need to step in to contain the enthusiasm of either party for an unrealistic amount of reparation.

In youth justice, young offenders may have to complete a certain number of hours of unpaid reparation work, or a specific task, as a requirement of their court order. The nature of this reparation can be discussed in the restorative meeting.

- If the victim doesn't want any practical reparation for themselves, ask if they might like to make suggestions for a task to benefit the wider community.

- If the offender is required as a condition of their order to undertake a fixed number of hours of reparation or community punishment, don't subvert the restorative process to fit this requirement. Direct reparation, if requested, could be just part of the total hours. Reparation is only restorative if it reflects the victim's wishes.

■ It may be necessary to stress that their ideas will be taken into account and that every effort will be made to follow through, but they may not be feasible when it comes to making practical arrangements.

■ Whatever the outcome, offer to provide feedback to the victim on how the reparation has gone.

## Contracts

A contract for reparation that the offender will fulfil/implement to make amends may be agreed. Written contracts are often unnecessary, but in some circumstances it can be useful to add a sense of formality or gravitas to the agreement, or to make a record if very specific reparation is agreed.

*'Would you like this written down?'*

*'This may get complicated; can we write this down so that we are all clear about what has been agreed?'*

It may include, for example, money or an offer for practical reparation.

Contracts may relate to behaviour rather than reparation. If there is a fear that problems may arise should the parties meet by chance in the community, the contract could establish what will happen ('we will carry on walking and ignore one another', or 'we will say "hi" but not expect to be friends', etc). The contract could state what will happen if the circumstances leading up to the offence are repeated.

> ⚠ *Don't be drawn into agreements for undeliverable goals; it is our responsibility to make sure that the commitment is viable.*

### CONTRACT WORDING

■ Take time to get the wording clear, and be sure that everyone understands and agrees.

- Add a disclaimer to the effect that the contract is for the participants, is voluntary and not enforceable.

- Have a space for everyone who is at the meeting to sign.

- If possible have copies of the contract for the participants to take home (using a photocopier, laptop or carbon paper).

### MONITORING THE CONTRACT

- Include in the contract who will monitor the honouring of each element of the contract (to ensure that the letter of apology has been written, compensation paid, etc.), ensuring that the arrangements are sound.

- Consider whether any particular documentation, receipts, signatures and witnesses are necessary.

- If you are signing to monitor an aspect of the contract, make sure that you follow it up diligently.

Think carefully before accepting responsibility yourself for money to be paid, considering whether you are the best person to undertake this task, and how you would manage it in practice.

> (!) *Failure to ensure that the offender honours his/her promises will re-victimise the victim.*

## Stage 5: Endings

The meeting is now entering its final stage, looking to the future, and how everyone wants things to be from now on.

*'What do you want to see come out of this meeting?'*

Victims will often say that what they wish for most is that the offender accepts the help they need to sort their life out and avoid hurting anyone else in the future.

*'How could this situation be dealt with differently another time?'*

## Summarising the achievements of the meeting

- At the end of the meeting, summarise what has been achieved.

It may be helpful to hear repeated an apology or other significant statement that was only said once. This may be a role
for the co-facilitator, who might find it helpful to take notes
during the meeting for this purpose.

*'Is there anything anyone wants to add?'*

- Explain the links between what happened at the meeting
and what happens next.

- Some restorative processes, specifically the referral order
and family group conference, have built in reviews.
There is no reason why a review might not be suggested
for other restorative meetings.

- Finally, thank everyone for their contribution.

   *'Thank you for giving up your time and engaging in the
   meeting.'*

## After the meeting

- After the meeting, offer refreshments and biscuits.

- Don't hurry everyone out.

- Decide before the meeting who will leave the room first,
and whether debriefing will be undertaken with each
party by both mediators, or one-to-one. If one party has
to wait, arrange for a colleague to look after them.

- Check everyone's satisfaction with the meeting, allowing each party individually time to reflect on their experience.

- Ask about any residual concerns or queries.

- Ask both parties if further information or contact is required. If it has been emotional, a friendly phone call to
check how they are doing might be welcomed in the
evening, with a home visit offered after a week or so, as
the implications of the experience start to sink in.

- Make sure that the offender is well supported after the meeting.[5]

- Explain that there will be a follow-up call or letter for evaluation, giving clear information about the procedures and reasons.

- Feed back immediately to the offender's caseworker.

### Provide the option for a follow-up session

If a wish is expressed to make contact with the scheme again, make sure that appropriate details are given.

In most cases the victim will feel that they have gained all that they might expect from a restorative meeting and will decline a follow-up session, although this can be offered if appropriate. Indirect contact (e.g. through letters or messages) can keep the communication alive, and either party may like to know how the other is doing. The decision to close the case should rest with the victim.

In the case of a referral order or family group conference where a review is built in to the process, it is more common for the victim to choose to meet the offender more than once. It can be powerful for them to perceive positive change in the offender over time.

- All parties should be contacted on closure of the case.

- Ensure that any support for either party that has been identified in the meeting is sourced and implemented (e.g. anger management, help with substance dependency, social services, etc.).

### Debriefing

- Once the parties have left, debrief with your co-facilitator if you have one. Critically examine how the meeting went:

  *'What went well?'*

  *'What could have been done differently?'*

---

5    Experience indicates that while many victims leave on a high note, offenders often feel down immediately after a restorative meeting.

- If a restorative meeting or visit is particularly stressful, talk to someone as soon as possible.

- In your report on a restorative intervention, reflect on and evaluate your practice. Sharing difficulties develops skills and knowledge for the team.

## Ongoing support

- Attend regular support or supervision meetings. This is essential to keep a check on good practice. Attend group support meetings to exchange ideas and best practice, and to share problems.

- Identify training that you feel would be helpful to you.

- Ask for individual supervision. Supervision offers an opportunity to discuss any issues causing you anxiety as soon as possible.

# 10

# SHUTTLE MEDIATION

Shuttle mediation starts as soon as you exchange any information between the parties, which may be during your first meetings and may continue throughout the whole process.

- Regardless of whether a restorative meeting takes place, the process of indirect or shuttle mediation begins as soon as you meet the victim or offender.

The mediation process is best viewed as a continuum, that may or may not lead to a face-to-face meeting.

Whilst it is recognised that a face-to-face meeting is the best scenario, shuttle mediation can sometimes be just as powerful. It is an excellent alternative if either one or both parties aren't prepared to meet (or your assessment is that a meeting isn't appropriate), but where they would like to communicate indirectly.

> (!) *Shuttle (indirect) mediation may be all that is required to satisfy the victim, and should not be considered inferior.*

Victims value communication, and our primary aim is to facilitate this. Victims should be able to enjoy the benefits of a restorative process even if they choose not to attend a meeting with 'their' offender, or if a face-to-face meeting is deemed inappropriate.

- When meeting with the victim, listen carefully to the issues they raise, and if you hear something you think could be important for the offender to hear and possibly respond to, ask permission to mention it to the offender. Give assurance that the information will be delivered with the utmost care and respect.

- Immediately after meeting the victim, make notes of this information.

- At a meeting with the victim(s) you may help them to write a list of questions for the offender, or decide what they might like to express. Unless you offer this, they may feel that it is 'a meeting or nothing'.

- Similarly, when meeting with the offender, listen for information that may be important for the victim. Assist them to understand the value of such information for victims. Treat it with respect.

> ⚠ *Always seek consent for exchange of information.*

## Letters

Letters may be a useful means of communication. Any letter from the offender to the victim must be acceptable to the victim.

- Check with the victim that they wish to receive a letter.

- Don't hand over sealed letters. It is important that the mediator or facilitator is aware of the contents of letters to ensure the emotional safety of the recipient.

Letters to victims should address the victims' needs. The letter has to be the offender's own, but any help that he or she needs should be available. Most victims prefer a hand-written letter.

- Don't post the letter; you need to know what state the victim is in. Arrange to bring the letter to them in person, and describe how it came to be written. Reassure them that it is the offender's own sentiments, and listen to their reaction. Encourage them to respond if they would like to.

> ⚠ *Letters can usefully be written by either party.*

# 11

# REFERRAL ORDERS AND PANELS

The Youth Justice and Criminal Evidence Act 1999 introduced the referral order. Referral panels are probably the most used restorative 'framework' in the UK. Arguably however they aren't fully restorative. Whilst the victim has a choice of whether to attend the panel, the offender has none, and may be compelled to meet their victim against their wishes. On the positive side, restorative justice is written into legislation for the first time, with a duty for Youth Offending Teams (YOTs) to deliver. For information on referral orders and panels, see the Youth Justice Board website www.yjb.gov.uk. For those managing the process:

- Don't allow volunteer training to be watered down or reduced in length or depth. If anything, panels with reluctant offenders can be more challenging than other restorative meetings.

- Build in training for panel advisors.

## The panel process

Referral orders make up a large proportion of a YOT's caseload, and can be an administrative headache. However, it is a key stage in a young person's offending career.

- Avoid turning panels into a sausage machine with several organised back-to-back. Allow time for each panel.

- Don't allow panels to become a 'rubber stamping' exercise, with the YOT or volunteers deciding what should go into the contract before the panel has even convened or the victim/offender has been consulted.

- Ensure that the place and timing of panels remains flexible to allow victims to attend if they wish.

Panel volunteers won't have met either party before facilitating the meeting, and will be going in 'cold'. Often no-one has met both parties prior to the panel. A separate assessment will be done for the offender by their case holder, and for the victim by a restorative justice or victim worker.

- If the victim would like to attend the panel, ensure that they are supported by the restorative justice or victim worker, who can greet them at the venue, sit with them during the meeting and then debrief them afterwards.

Panels with victims and reluctant offenders can be tricky. However, if handled carefully, they can have a surprising and positive result all round. The restorative process has a transformative power of its own, and it is more satisfying to get a good outcome from an unpromising beginning. However, they can also go dreadfully wrong and end up being re-victimising for the victim.

- Have a robust risk assessment process in place for considering whether it is safe for the victim to attend.

- Prepare the victim thoroughly for what to expect.

Don't jump to a decision to exclude the victim from the panel. Youth Justice Board guidance states that 'only in exceptional cases is the victim to be denied attending panel'. When handled carefully they can work.

- Don't have anyone attending the panel (e.g. a victim supporter) who hasn't been visited and assessed first.

- The restorative justice or victim worker may like to meet the offender prior to the panel, so that a more rounded risk assessment can be made.

- Consider having an experienced restorative justice facilitator to run the restorative portion of the panel when a victim is present, if it is likely to be difficult.

- Be particularly rigorous at negotiating groundrules, and stress that anyone can call for a break at any time during the panel.

Some YOTs have a separate restorative meeting outside the panel process in cases where the victim hopes to attend. This can be a flexible way of working and should be considered. However, if it is done in every case it undermines the role of the panel volunteer and prevents them from hearing directly from victims.

- If the victim would like some involvement in the panel process, but doesn't wish to meet the offender face-to-face (or where this is assessed to be inappropriate), consider inviting them to a special 'panel' without the offender present. This gives them a sense of being heard, and provides the panel with a more balanced picture of the offence.

- If the victim wishes to attend but is prevented (e.g. they live some distance away), consider turning the panel into a video conference, or filming the part that the victim would have attended and showing them the footage afterwards.

- If there is no victim involvement, ensure that the victim perspective is central to the process. Don't allow the panel to skate over it without challenging the young person to consider the effects of their actions and accept responsibility for the harm they caused.

- Consider surrogate victims. If a young person assaults a police officer, perhaps a member of the YOT's final warning team can attend if the officer is prevented.

Refresher training for panel volunteers could cover practice issues:

- Do you over-dominate the panel?
- Is there good use of silence?
- What are helpful lines of questions?
- Are your panels becoming formulistic?

Refresher training with good use of role-plays can be productive.

## Referral order contracts

- Don't come to the panel with a clear idea of what 'you want' in the contract.

- Avoid formulas for the number of hours of reparation per month. Try to keep the process flexible and creative. An apology, gift or offer of a letter may be reparation enough.

- Consider reparation 'tasks' rather than numbers of hours (e.g. weeding round the hall that was burgled).

- Be well informed about opportunities for interventions outside the YOT which could be included in the order.

## Referral order reviews and sign-offs

Unlike other restorative processes, panels have regular reviews, usually set at three-month intervals. In some cases, the young person and the volunteers build a positive and constructive relationship, which helps to hold the offender through the period of the order. Victims may wish to attend reviews, and can enjoy seeing the young person progress through their order.

- Be flexible about timing of reviews, to accommodate the victim.

- Don't miss out or water down the review or sign-off process.

Consider using 'show and tell'. The young person could prepare in advance a display (photos, a poster, video, etc.) of the work, including reparation, that they have been doing during their order.

# 12

# RECORDING AND EVALUATION

- Keep offender and victim details separately.

- Keep all written information in a secure place.

- Ensure that your agency has a written policy about storage of confidential information: for example, at what stage written or electronic records are destroyed.

Measures designed to evaluate successful outcomes of restorative processes need to be led by participants' standards of success, not simply those of the agency. It may be helpful to design regular research providing a snapshot to keep ourselves updated with what clients are thinking.

## Feedback to referrers, magistrates and the media

- It is good practice to inform the courts, magistrates and other partners about the success of your restorative justice project, particularly highlighting outcomes for victims.

- Consider what is appropriate to share without breaching confidentiality.

Good media stories about restorative justice help balance the negativity of most crime reporting, and encourage others to get involved. Individual case studies are always powerful, and clients who have recently been through a restorative process may be glad to help your project in this way. Sharing

their experience through the media can be part of their healing.

- Carefully brief reporters, who may want to focus more on the harm than the repair.

- You may come under pressure to allow filming of a restorative meeting. Give careful thought before agreeing. Participants will be aware that there is a camera there and it will definitely change the nature of the meeting.

## Professional development

Basic training in restorative justice in line with the latest standards should be followed up with development and supervision.

- Ask about possibilities for accreditation or for qualifications such as NVQ.

# Appendix

## Prompt sheet for restorative meetings

Arrive at venue. Seat participants as planned for maximum communication and comfort.

### Stage 1: Introductions and groundrules

- Mobile phones to be switched off.

- Welcome and introduction of those present.

- Health and safety and domestic notices.

- Establish groundrules:

    - everyone will be given an opportunity to have their say

    - listen respectfully if someone is speaking

    - don't interrupt, or use abusive or threatening language or behaviour

    - take time out if you need to

    - be open and speak truthfully

    - respect confidentiality.

- Set the scene:

    - relationship of the meeting to formal processes

    - focus the meeting on the particular incident

    - participation is voluntarily (other than in referral order panel meeting)

    - be clear that the offender accepts responsibility.

## Stage 2: Hearing everyone's stories

- Outline the structure of the meeting.
- Draw out everyone's story:
  - thoughts and feelings at the time
  - thoughts and feelings since
  - who has been affected
  - what have been the emotional, physical and material consequences.
- Hear from each of the supporters.

## Stage 3: Addressing issues and needs

- Identify specific needs arising from the offence.
- Address the victim's questions.
- Invite the offender to respond.

## Stage 4: Reflecting on ways of repairing the harm

- Discuss and agree specific outcomes for victim and offender.
- Consider a contract and monitoring of the contract.

## Stage 5: Endings

- Ask what everyone wants to see coming out of the meeting.
- Summarise the achievements of the meeting.
- Remind participants about any follow-up arrangements.
- Thank everyone for their contribution.
- Don't forget to debrief with your co-facilitator.

# Resources

Graef, R. (2001) *Why Restorative Justice?* London: Calouste
Gulbenkian Foundation.

Home Office (2004) *Best Practice Guidance for Restorative Practitioners.*
London: Home Office. Available at
www.homeoffice.gov.uk/documents/rj_bestpractice.pdf?version
=1, accessed on 5 November 2007.

Hopkins, B. (2004) *Just Schools: A Whole School Approach in Restorative
Justice.* London: Jessica Kingsley Publishers.

Hoyle, C. (2002) 'Securing Restorative Justice for the
"Non-Participating" Victim.' In C. Hoyle and R. Young (eds)
*New Visions of Crime Victims.* Oxford: Hart Publishing,
pp.97–132.

Hoyle, C., Young, R. and Hill, R. (2002) *Proceed with Caution: An
Evaluation of the Thames Valley Police Initiative in Restorative
Cautioning.* York: Joseph Rowntree Foundation.

Leibmann, M. (2007) *Restorative Justice: How it Works.* London: Jessica
Kingsley Publishers.

O'Connell, T., Wachtel, B. and Wachtel, T. (1999) *Conferencing
Handbook: The New Real Justice Training Manual.* Pipersville, PA:
The Piper's Press.

Restorative Justice Consortium (2004) *Principles of Restorative Justice.*
Available at www.restorativejustice.org.uk/?Resources:Best_
Practice:Principles, accessed on 5 November 2007.

Taylor, J. (2004) *Crime against Retail and Manufacturing Premises:
Findings from the 2002 Commercial Victimisation Survey.* London:
Home Office. Available at www.homeoffice.gov.uk/rds/
pdfs04/r259.pdf, accessed on 5 November 2007.

Youth Justice Board (2003a) *Key Elements of Effective Practise: Swift
Administration of Justice.* London: Youth Justice Board.

Youth Justice Board (2003b) *Key Elements of Effective Practice:
Restorative Justice.* London: Youth Justice Board.

## Online resources

**Family Rights Group (Family Group Conferences)**
www.frg.org.uk
The Family Rights Group is a charity in England and Wales that advises parents and other family members whose children are involved with or require social care services. Their website provides a description of the family group conference model and contains information about local and regional family group conference groups and networks.

**Home Office** www.homeoffice.gov.uk (type 'Restorative Justice' in the search box)
The Home Office website provides information about restorative justice, published guidance for practitioners and trainers, links to government policies and press updates.

**Restorative Justice Consortium** www.restorativejustice.org.uk
The Restorative Justice Consortium (RJC) is an infrastructure organisation for restorative justice in England and Wales. The RJC provides support and networking opportunities for restorative justice practitioners and trainers as well as groups and organisations interested in using restorative justice. The website has a wealth of information and resources including best practice guidance, news and events in the world of restorative justice.

**Restorative Justice Online (part of Prison Fellowship International)** www.restorativejustice.org
Prison Fellowship International's website features news about restorative justice projects worldwide, including details of publications, conferences, events, research and jobs.

**Transforming Conflict (The National Centre for Restorative Justice in Youth Setting)** www.transformingconflict.org
Transforming Conflict is a national organisation that offers training, consultancy and support for restorative justice in youth settings. The website provides information about what a restrative approach in such settings entails, in addition to details of events, training and resources.

**Youth Justice Board** www.yjb.gov.uk
The Youth Justice Board (YJB) oversees the youth justice system in England and Wales. The YJB website provides details and guidance on all aspects of restorative practice in youth justice. The Directory of Emerging Practice is a web-based resource for practitioners who can share good practice online.

# Index